THE ONLY WAY TO BE GOOD

A STUDY OF ROMANS

BIBLE STUDIES TO IMPACT THE LIVES OF ORDINARY PEOPLE

Written by Dorothy Russell

The Word Worldwide

CHRISTIAN FOCUS

For details of our titles visit us on our website
www.christianfocus.com

ISBN 1-85792-950-0

Copyright © WEC International

Published in 2004 by
Christian Focus Publications, Geanies House,
Fearn, Ross-shire, IV20 ITW, Scotland
and
WEC International, Bulstrode, Oxford Road,
Gerrards Cross, Bucks, SL9 8SZ

Cover design by Alister MacInnes

Printed and bound by J W Arrowsmith, Bristol

CONTENTS

PREFACE 4
KEY THOUGHTS IN ROMANS 5
INTRODUCTORY STUDY 6

QUESTIONS AND NOTES

STUDY 1 – HOW DO I MEASURE UP? 8
STUDY 2 – FREE ... FOR ALL 12
STUDY 3 – IF CHRIST HAD NOT BEEN OBEDIENT...? 16
STUDY 4 – DEAD ... AND ALIVE! 20
STUDY 5 – HELP! 23
STUDY 6 – WHO IS IN CONTROL? 27
STUDY 7 – WHAT ABOUT THE JEWS? 31
STUDY 8 – 'LORD, CHANGE ME!' 34
STUDY 9 – BLUEPRINT FOR DAILY LIVING 38
STUDY 10 – REAL PEOPLE, LIKE US 41

ANSWER GUIDE

STUDY 1 47
STUDY 2 48
STUDY 3 49
STUDY 4 50
STUDY 5 51
STUDY 6 52
STUDY 7 53
STUDY 8 54
STUDY 9 55
STUDY 10 56

PREFACE

GEARED FOR GROWTH

'Where there's LIFE there's GROWTH:
Where there's GROWTH there's LIFE.'

WHY GROW a study group?

Because as we study the Bible and share together we can

* learn to combat loneliness, depression, staleness, frustration, and other problems
* get to understand and love each other
* become responsive to the Holy Spirit's dealing and obedient to God's Word

and that's GROWTH.

How do you GROW a study group?

* Just start by asking a friend to join you and then aim at expanding your group.
* Study the set portions daily (they are brief and easy: no catches).
* Meet once a week to discuss what you find.
* Befriend others, both Christians and non Christians, and work away together

see how it GROWS!

WHEN you GROW ...

This will happen at school, at home, at work, at play, in your youth group, your student fellowship, women's meetings, mid-week meetings, churches and communities,

you'll be REACHING THROUGH TEACHING

KEY THOUGHTS IN ROMANS

INTRODUCTORY
STUDY: The gospel reveals how God puts people right with Himself (Rom. 1:17). It is through faith from beginning to end.

STUDY 1:   God's anger is revealed from Heaven against all sin and evil (Rom. 1:18; 2:11). God judges everyone by the same standard.

STUDY 2:   But now God's way of putting people right with Himself has been revealed (Rom. 3:21, 22). It has nothing to do with the law. God puts people right through their faith in Jesus Christ.

STUDY 3:   Just as all people were made sinners as a result of the disobedience of one man (Rom. 5:19), in the same way they will all be put right with God as a result of the obedience of one Man.

STUDY 4:   Count on the fact that you are dead so far as sin is concerned (Rom. 6:11), but living in fellowship with God through Jesus Christ.

STUDY 5:   Even though the desire to do good is in me, I am not able to do it (Rom. 7:18).

STUDY 6:   Those who live as the Spirit tells them to have their minds controlled by what the Spirit wants (Rom. 8:5).

STUDY 7:   If the Jews abandon their unbelief, they will be put back in the place where they were (Rom. 11:23), for God is able to do that.

STUDY 8:   God transforms you inwardly by a complete change of your mind (Rom. 12:2), then you will be able to know the will of God.

STUDY 9:   We must always aim at those things that bring peace, and that help to strengthen one another (Rom. 14:19).

STUDY 10: May God, our source of peace, be with you all (Rom. 15:33).

Write out the text for each week and try to memorize it.

INTRODUCTORY STUDY

PUTTING WRONGS RIGHT

The central theme of the book of Romans is expressed in these words from chapter I verse 17:

> 'The Gospel reveals how God puts people right with Himself; it is through **faith** from beginning to end.'

Learn this by heart if you can, and refer to it constantly during the 10 week study.

* * *

Read Romans 1:1-8 in several different versions, if possible.

What can you find out about: Paul?
The Good News (gospel)?
The Lord Jesus Christ?
The believers in Rome?

Share together anything else you may know about Paul, the Good News, the Lord Jesus Christ, and the believers in Rome.
Read chapter 1:1-8 again.

* * *

Read Romans 1:9-15.
What might Paul reply, if he were interviewed in the following way?

INTERVIEWER: Paul, you say you serve God. Just how do you do this?
INTERVIEWER: What is your greatest wish at the moment?
INTERVIEWER: If some people in Rome are already Christians, what good will a visit from you do?
INTERVIEWER: Have you never thought of going to Rome before?

Now look up Acts 28:14-24, 30 and 31, and find out how Paul did arrive in Rome – not quite the way he had expected!
Although his circumstances were unforeseen, did he do what he had planned?
Which verses tell us this?

TAKE TIME TO THINK:
- What does the word 'gospel' mean?
- Take a pencil and paper, and write down what you would say to someone who asked, 'What exactly is the gospel that you talk about? And what has it got to do with me?'
- Share your written answers, and then check them with what Paul said in Romans 1:16-17 (use several versions).
- Can you say the words from the beginning of this study by heart yet?
- Was this some new idea of Paul's? (see Hab. 2:4)

* * *

QUESTIONS FOR DISCUSSION IN SMALL GROUPS:
A. 'Christian preachers are forever telling us that we're all worms and sinners and evil kinds of people. Where do they get that idea? Not everyone is a killer or a law-breaker.'

B. 'I am a Christian, and can honestly say I live a good life, and always have. I love the Lord Jesus, and I just don't feel I have any sins to confess. Is this normal when you've been brought up in a Christian home?'

C. 'In our street there is a man who bashed up his wife so much that she had to get a divorce; and there's a woman who spends all her time helping people – she doesn't go to church but she's a marvellous person; then there's our family – a mixed bunch and we have our hassles, but we get along OK most of the time.'

'Now ... how can you say God is just if He judges all these people by the same standard? Compared with the wife-basher, I'm a saint!'

STUDY 1

HOW DO I MEASURE UP?

QUESTIONS

Read the **KEY THOUGHT** at least once each day this week.
KEY THOUGHT: 'God's anger is revealed from Heaven against all sin and evil. God judges everyone by the same standard.'

DAY 1   *Romans 1:18-25.*
a) From earliest times God has given man evidence that He exists and that He is a powerful God. What is the evidence?

b) What does this passage say about people who do not acknowledge God or thank Him for His care?

DAY 2   *Romans 1:26-32.*
a) Discuss how true a picture this is of today's society.

b) What is the reason given in verse 28 for this kind of life style?

DAY 3   *Romans 2:1-16.*
a) What should be our response to God's kindness and patience (v. 4)?

b) What is the standard by which God judges everyone? (Matt. 5:48)

QUESTIONS (contd.)

DAY 4 *Romans 2:17-24.*

a) Which verse summarizes what Paul is saying here to the Jews?

b) Look up the story in Luke 18:9-14. What did the Pharisee not realise?

DAY 5 *Romans 2:25-29.*

a) What was the physical sign that a man was a Jew?

b) What does Paul say is the mark of a real Jew?

c) What does God look for in people who go to church today? (Look up Jer. 31:33 and 2 Cor. 5:17.)

DAY 6 *Romans 3:1-8; 9:4-5.*

a) What privileges did God give the Jews?

b) What does chapter 3:3 tell us about the Jews?

c) How would you link this up with yesterday's questions?

DAY 7 *Romans 3:9-20; Psalm 14:2-3.*

a) What is the main teaching of these verses? (see also v. 23)

b) What was God's purpose in giving the Law? (v. 20)

'God judges everyone by the same standard.'
What is God's standard? It is ABSOLUTE PERFECTION.... how do **you** measure up?

Test yourself with this quiz:

Have you ever been dishonest or told a lie?
Have you ever broken a promise?
Have you ever had an unkind thought? Or an impure one?
Can you think of a time when you have failed to do something you should have done?
When did you last feel resentful, offended or critical? Have you ever been unwilling to say 'sorry'?

Need we go any further ...?
If you are still not sure how you measure up to God's standard, read Colossians chapter 3 at home prayerfully.
God's word tells us, 'Whoever breaks one commandment is guilty of breaking them all' (Jas. 2:10).

* * *

Our study this week has shown us 3 types of people:

1. 'The baddies' Chapter 1:18-32 (1st and 2nd days)
Turn on the news, open your morning paper, and you will find them. Talk to any social worker, and he will confirm that these verses are all too true.

Society today says a man may not be responsible for the crime he commits – perhaps his circumstances are to blame – but God says: 'The heart is deceitful above all things, and desperately corrupt' (Jer. 17:9).

God holds each individual responsible for the way he lives his life (see vv. 20-21) and anything which falls short of God's standard of perfection is SIN – that's what God calls it.

2. 'The goodies' Chapter 2:1-16 (3rd day)
We all know people who are decent, honest folk, and who do a lot of good in this world, but have no time for God and His church.

God judges everyone by the same standard, as we have learned, and that standard is absolute perfection, to be found only in Jesus Christ.

So even the good-living, moral people, when they stand before God on Judgment Day, will find that their lives do not measure up to His standard. God is perfectly fair and He offers the same way of salvation to all – identification with the sinless Lord Jesus Christ.

3. 'The religious people' Chapter 2:17-29 (4th and 5th days)
Jungle Doctor in one of his fables, tells how Goat wanted to become a lion! He asked his friend Monkey how this could be done. Monkey thought hard.

'Mm. For a goat to become a lion,' he said,
'he must DO what lions do,
GO where lions go,
SAY what lions say,
and EAT what lions eat.'

However, although poor Goat followed this excellent advice most meticulously, he remained a goat.
(Unfortunately, when he actually WENT where lions went, he became, not a lion – but a lion's dinner!)
Jungle Doctor gave the answer to his riddle:

'For a goat to become a lion,
he would have to be born again as a lion cub.'

Can you see the parallel?

* * *

Read together Romans 3:22 and praise God for its truth.

STUDY 2

FREE ... FOR ALL

QUESTIONS

KEY THOUGHT (*read each day*): 'But now God's way of putting people right with Himself has been revealed. It has nothing to do with Law.... God puts people right through their faith in Jesus Christ.'

DAY 1   *Romans 3:21-26; Titus 3:4-5*
a) Write down in one sentence what last week's study was about.

b) Since the Law cannot make us right with God, what can?

DAY 2   *Romans 3:27-31; Deuteronomy 6:4-6.*
a) What might we be tempted to boast about?

b) If we are justified by faith in Christ, why should we not just forget about the Law? (Matt. 5:17)

DAY 3   *Romans 4:1-5; Genesis 15:1-6.*
a) How was it that Abraham was put right with God? Does this agree with this week's key thought?

b) What is the difference between wages and a gift?

DAY 4   *Romans 4:6-12; Galatians 3:6-9.*
a) How can a person become truly happy (or blessed)?

QUESTIONS (contd.)

b) Ask yourself if you have the kind of happiness described here.

c) Who are the people who can share the same blessing as Abraham?

DAY 5 *Romans 4:13-17* (Living Bible helpful here).
a) If we insist that we must try to be good enough, to be accepted by God – what is the result?

b) How is it that Abraham is like the father of us, even though we are not Jews?

DAY 6 *Romans 4:18-21; Hebrews 11:11-12.*
a) What can you learn from Abraham that could help you in your daily life?

b) Why was it surprising that Abraham believed God in the matter mentioned here?

DAY 7 *Romans 4:21-25.*
a) When God accepted Abraham because of his faith, what further purpose had He in mind?

b) Why did Jesus have to die?

c) Why was He raised to life again?

NOTES

Father and young son are walking. They come to a fast flowing river:

FATHER: Now son, it's too wide and deep for you to get over but I'll take you on my shoulders and carry you across.

SON: But Dad, I'm good at maths at school, I can work out how far it is to the other side, and just how long it would take to wade across.

FATHER: If you estimate how deep it is too, you'll find it's way out of your depth!

SON: Well, I'm the best swimmer in our class! I could try swimming. I can do two lengths of the pool.

FATHER: Son, this isn't a swimming pool! You would be swept crashing on to the rocks. No, the only way is for me to carry you, and steady myself with my strong stick.

SON: Wait a minute – what about using some fallen logs as a raft? You know how clever I am at making things with my hands. I could strap a few logs together with some cord – look, I even have some in my pocket. I'm not a Boy Scout for nothing!

FATHER: Can't you see, lad, that no matter how good you are at maths, or swimming, or bushcraft this river is too deep, too strong, and too wide for you to get across by your own efforts?

SON: Well ... that's what you say. But I still think I could try.

FATHER: I love you too much for that, son. There's only **one way** to get to the other side. Just hang on to me and trust me. I'll get you across.

SON: That almost seems too easy! But of course I trust you, Dad. Ready for me to jump up?

* * *

JUST THINK –
God did not decide He could only accept:

- those who obey the Law
- those who have been circumcised
- those who are the cream of the intellectuals
- those who spend their lives helping others
- those who have been brought up in a Christian home
- those with a high income
- those who keep in good health
- those who have never committed any serious crimes
- those who go to church regularly
- those from a particular cultural background
- or those who have proved themselves worthy of His love.

Quite the opposite!
Jesus said, 'I came, not to call the righteous, but sinners to repentance.'

Steve Schiffman, who has written the book 'Once a Thief', was a no-hoper, a pusher of heroin, a target of underworld assassination attempts, a disciple of Satan. His life story makes chilling reading.
Yet God revealed Himself to Steve through the love of Christian people who shared the Word; he accepted Christ, and God accepted him, and forgave and completely wiped out all his sordid past.

* * *

Read together Ephesians 2:8-9.

STUDY 3

IF CHRIST HAD *NOT* BEEN OBEDIENT...?

QUESTIONS

Read this **KEY THOUGHT** every day: 'Just as all people were made sinners as a result of the disobedience of one man, in the same way they will all be put right with God as a result of the obedience of one Man.'

DAY 1 *Romans 5:1-2; Isaiah 26:3.*
a) What is the immediate result of coming into a right relationship with God.

b) Because we have accepted what Jesus has done for us, what can we confidently look forward to? (also I John 3:2)

DAY 2 *Romans 5:3-5.*
a) Why can we even rejoice in our sufferings and problems? Have you tried looking at your problems this way?

b) What is said here about the Holy Spirit?

DAY 3 *Romans 5:6-8, 10.*
a) What words are used here to describe us before we came into a right relationship with God?

b) How would you answer a person who said, 'I'm not good enough to be a Christian?'

QUESTIONS (contd.)

DAY 4   *Romans 5:9-11; 1 John 4:10.*
a) Once again, Paul states what Jesus has done for us through His death. What is it?

b) Stop here, and read verses 1-11 again, and thank the Lord Jesus with all your heart.

DAY 5   *Romans 5:12-14.*
a) God created everything perfect (Gen. 1:27-31). How then did sin enter the human race?

b) What automatically followed sin? (Gen. 2:17)

DAY 6   *Romans 5:15-17.*
a) What two things are being contrasted here?

b) What are the results of these two things?

DAY 7   *Romans 5:18-21.*
a) What happened when sin increased?

b) Look at the title of this study. If Christ had not been obedient, and had not died on the cross, how would this affect you today?

NOTES

This chapter gives us some pretty strong words to describe people who do not belong to Jesus Christ. Remember them?

Utterly helpless
Powerless
Sinful
Wicked
Ungodly
Enemies of God.

If Christ had not been obedient, this is how God would see us today.
Look back to the key thought for Study I.
Do you remember what God's standard is?

In contrast, this chapter gives us some tremendous words to describe the blessings God has given to those who do belong to Jesus Christ. Remember them?

Peace with God
Joy, even in times of suffering
Hope of sharing the glory of God
Love of God in our hearts
Gift of the Holy Spirit
Forgiveness
Reconciliation.

If Christ had not been obedient, none of these blessings would be ours.

The following words are used in various translations of this chapter. List them in the appropriate columns.

- free gift, sin, death, grace, judgment, justification, righteousness, punishment, trespass, condemnation, eternal life, forgiveness, mercy, penalty, acquittal.

ADAM BROUGHT:	CHRIST BRINGS:

One of the exquisite words to which the Bible introduces us is GRACE. Perhaps it is best defined as: 'God's undeserved mercy to man'.

After studying Romans chapter 5, we may catch a glimpse of how precious the grace of God is. No matter how enormous the problem of sin is in our world, God's grace is always greater, and freely available to those who come to Him.

> He giveth more grace when the burdens grow greater,
> He sendeth more strength when the labours increase,
> To added affliction He addeth His mercy,
> To multiplied trials, His multiplied peace.
>
> When we have exhausted our store of endurance,
> When our strength has failed e'er the day is half done,
> When we reach the end of our hoarded resources,
> Our Father's forgiving has only begun.
>
> His love has no limits, His grace has no measure,
> His power no boundary known unto men,
> But out of His infinite riches in Jesus
> He giveth, and giveth ... and giveth again.

Spend a little time when you go home today, looking up the following verses which will give you more insight into the meaning of this beautiful word 'GRACE'.

1 Corinthians 15:10
2 Corinthians 12:7-9
Ephesians 1:6-8
Ephesians 2:4-7

STUDY 4

DEAD ... AND ALIVE!

QUESTIONS

KEY THOUGHT: 'Think of yourselves as **dead** so far as sin is concerned, but **living** in fellowship with God through Jesus Christ.'

DAY 1 *Romans 6:1-4.*
a) Look back to chapter 5:20. What argument did people put forward about sin and God's grace?

b) What is Paul's answer?

DAY 2 *Romans 6:4-7.*
a) Becoming a Christian means identification (being united) with Christ. How does a dead person react to sin and temptation?

b) What does identification with 1) Christ's death, and 2) His resurrection, mean to us?

DAY 3 *Romans 6:8-11.*
a) What is said here about Christ and death?

b) How are we to be 'dead' and 'alive' at the same time?

Verses 1-11 have been teaching us the truths we need to grasp, and the remaining verses tell us the practical application of them.

QUESTIONS (contd.)

DAY 4 *Romans 6:12-14.*
a) As Christians, what must we not do?

b) There is only one way to make sure we don't do these things. What is it? (see also Rom. 12:1)

DAY 5 *Romans 6:15-16.*
a) What picture does Paul use here to show the power that sin can have on a life?

b) Give a present day example of this kind of power.

DAY 6 *Romans 6:17-19.*
a) What is the vitally important truth that Paul hammers home in this chapter? (vv. 6, 7, 10, 18, 22)

b) Have you experienced this in your own life?

c) What positive action does Paul again urge us to take?

DAY 7 *Romans 6:20-23.*
a) Those who are slaves of sin are free from   ....
and the result is   ....
Those who are slaves of God are free from   ....
and the result is   ....
b) Read verse 23 several times, then put it in your own words.

NOTES

Let's recap –

Study 1 told us of God's holy anger against all sin, and His judgment upon it.

Study 2 revealed God's remedy for sin the only remedy – faith in Jesus Christ.

Study 3 moved on to show the blessings and benefits enjoyed by those who have put their faith in Christ.

Now **Study 4** goes a step further.

Not only do Christians enjoy the benefits of Christ's death, they also experience a new kind of life. This new life includes freedom from the mastery of sin in daily life. Sin's power to hurt still remains, but its power to dominate is overthrown. The title of a book by Jon Braun puts this rather neatly. It is called, *It ain't gonna reign no more.*

* * *

Imagine a young fellow, Jim, having a humdrum kind of job working for a boss named Mr Black. One day he sees an advertisement for a much better paid and more interesting job, and applies for it. He is interviewed by Mr White, gets the job, and gives notice to his former boss. He has now finished working for Mr Black, that contract has come to an end; and he starts work for Mr. White.

A few months later there is a knock at his door. There stands Mr Black.

'I want you to do a job for me,' he says.

But Jim replies, 'I don't work for you any longer, Sir. I've signed a new contract to work for Mr White.'

'Oh,' says Mr Black, 'but you used to work for me, and now I've come to demand that you do what I ask.'

'Too bad,' says Jim. 'You have no authority to demand anything. I have a new boss, and I'll only take orders from him. He's a far better boss than you are, and I enjoy this job much more. So I have no intention of doing what you ask.'

Mr. Black hasn't a leg to stand on, has he?

And that, says Paul, is exactly how it is with Sin which tries to dominate the Christian. It hasn't a leg to stand on!

Sin is no longer our boss, we are under new management since we changed over to Christ. So when Sin tempts us, we can remind ourselves that we don't have to give into it, but that Christ, our new Master, can give us power and authority to resist.

Our ability to overcome Sin depends on the closeness of our relationship with Christ.

STUDY 5

HELP!

QUESTIONS

KEY THOUGHT: (*It is most important to read it every day*) 'Even though the desire to do good is in me, I am not able to do it'

DAY 1 *Romans 7:1-3.*
a) When two people take a marriage vow, how long does that vow bind them for?

b) What happens if one partner dies?

DAY 2 *Romans 7:4-6.*
a) Because the Christian is united to Christ, what has Christ's death freed him from?

b) Read Deuteronomy 5:7-22 and Jeremiah 31:31-34. Where was the new covenant (or law) to be written? What does this mean?

DAY 3 *Romans 7:7-11.*
a) If there were no law, or rules for living, could a man be accused of doing wrong?

b) Read Exodus 20:1-17. Which commandment does Paul say he found difficult to keep? Which do you find most difficult?

QUESTIONS (contd.)

DAY 4   *Romans 7:12-13; Galatians 3:21-25.*
a) What can you find out about the law from these verses?

b) If God's law is good and right why do we not keep it perfectly?

DAY 5   *Romans 7:14-20* (you may have to read this several times!).
a) What does Paul find himself doing?

b) What can he not do?

c) What explanation of the conflict is given in Galatians 5:17?

DAY 6   *Romans 7:21-25.*
a) Look at verse 22. Does this indicate that Paul had this struggle before or after he became a Christian?

b) Which verse gives the glorious answer to this problem? What is that answer?

DAY 7   *Read the whole of Romans 7 again.*
a) What has God given to show man His perfect standard?

b) What happens when man faces up to this standard?

c) What is the Christian's desire? Can he do this in his own strength?

NOTES

Sinai is shaking. Lightning is flashing, smoke clouds are billowing around the sacred mountain. God is speaking to Moses, and God's finger is writing in stone the Ten Commandments – ten laws, ten rules by which man is to live.

These rules for successful living are for all peoples of all times. They have never been changed, amended or revoked. They are not out of date for the purpose for which God gave them. They are for us today. And yet I will shock you by saying that God never meant or expected that man could keep the Ten Commandments.

Then why did God give them, if He did not expect us to observe them? Because they are a mirror. We look into them and realise how far short we have come of God's standard of holy and righteous living. The moral law becomes a mirror for our souls, and reveals us as being guilty of breaking the law of God. It also drives us to the cross; that is, it teaches us to seek our salvation in Jesus Christ and not in our own efforts to keep the Law.

(Quoted from an article by Billy Graham in *Decision* magazine).

* * *

This chapter points out the essential difference between being 'religious' and being a child of God through Jesus Christ.

RELIGION (and there are many religions) can fill our minds with great and noble thoughts, but
RELIGION cannot show us how to achieve our aim.
RELIGION can make us miserable because our thoughts condemn our behaviour, but
RELIGION offers no comfort in our distress.
RELIGION is man trying to live by the Law, but constantly failing, constantly frustrated.

Can you identify with Paul's heart-cry here?

Can you agree with him when he says, 'Even though the desire to do good is in me, I am not able to do it'?

Peter discovered this. After asserting that he would stick with Jesus through thick and thin, he later denied three times that he even knew Him.

In the musical, 'The Witness', Peter sings these lovely words when the resurrected Christ asks him, 'Peter, do you love Me?'

'I love you, Lord,
And you know I always meant to do things right.
I love you, Lord,

When I think of how I've failed you, I could cry.
And when I hear you calling me
I want to run and hide,
Yet you know
I love you so.

'I love you, Lord,
Although I know my heart may not seem true.
I love you, Lord,
And I've prayed for one more chance to prove I do.
I want to leave the past behind
And feel your smile again,
Oh Lord, you know
I love you so.
I love you so.'

To sum up this remarkable chapter, we could put it like this:

- Without a set of rules – man could do as he pleased.
- The rule says, 'shoplifting is an offence',
    yet many people shoplift.
    They don't want to obey the law.

- When a person becomes a Christian,
    he **wants** to do what is right,
        but oh dear! he finds he hasn't the power to do it.
        Things keep going wrong.

This is the dilemma of Romans chapter 7.
But fortunately this story is '... to be continued.'
This is *not* the way God has planned for us to live as Christians.
Look out for another exciting episode next week!

STUDY 6

WHO IS IN CONTROL?

QUESTIONS

KEY THOUGHT (*try reading it aloud each day*): 'Those who live as the Spirit tells them to have their minds controlled by what the Spirit wants.'

DAY 1 *Romans 8:1-4.*
a) Which of these verses is a direct answer to Romans 7:24?

b) What can we learn about each of the three persons of the Godhead from this passage? (i.e. Father, Son, Spirit)

DAY 2 *Romans 8:5-11.*
a) People are divided into two groups in verse 5. What are they?

b) What different results do these two lifestyles produce?

c) Compare the end of verse 9 with I John 5:12. What is the difference?

DAY 3 *Romans 8:12-17.*
a) What is the status of those who are led by the Spirit of God?

b) Who tells us that this is so?

QUESTIONS (contd.)

DAY 4 *Romans 8:17-23.*
a) What comfort is there here for the Christian who is suffering?

b) What is all creation waiting for? (see also Gen. 3:17-18; Rev. 21:1)

DAY 5 *Romans 8:23-27; Revelation 21:3-4.*
a) What is the glorious hope that the Christian has?

b) Who helps us to pray?

c) Have you discovered any new thoughts in these verses?

DAY 6 *Romans 8:28-30.*
a) Give an example of verse 28 from your own experience if you can, or one you have read about.

b) The Living Bible ends verse 28 '... if we love God and are fitting into his plans.' What is God's plan for every child of His?

DAY 7 *Romans 8:31-39.*
a) If God is for us, who can be against us?

b) Who can condemn us if we are in Christ?

c) Who can separate us from the love of Christ?

d) Pause here, and thank God with all your heart for the truth of verses 38 and 39.

NOTES

The contrast shown in this chapter between those who live as human nature tells them to, and those who live as the Spirit tells them to, is staggering!

Do you really believe it is so important for **you** to be controlled by the Spirit of God in everything you do?

How does the Spirit get control?

It has to be by a deliberate action on your part. You have to hand over to Him the keys to every room in your life, be willing to submit to His promptings, begin each day by asking, 'Lord how do you want me to fill the moments of this day?' You must be prepared to say, when there's a choice to be made, 'Not my will, but yours be done.'

- Are you scared to do this?
- Afraid you might have to give up something you enjoy?
- Not sure what might happen?
- Afraid of what people would say?
- Think it's not very practical?
- Have you a sneaking suspicion that you can really make a better job of running your own life than God could?

* * *

Just take a look at the long list of benefits for those who let God the Holy Spirit run their lives:

There is no more struggling and frustration in life. (v. 2)
Their minds are perfectly controlled. (v. 5)
They have a full and satisfying life here and now. (v. 6)
God's peace is available to them in every situation. (v. 6)
They are God's sons and heirs. (v. 17)
They will inherit the blessings and the glory in eternity. (v. 17)
Prayer becomes a joy instead of a duty. (v. 26)
In whatever situation they find themselves, God is always working for their good. (v. 28)
With God on their side, they can stand up to anything. (v. 31)
They have overwhelming victory through Christ. (v. 37)
Nothing, absolutely nothing in this world or the next, can separate them from God's love. (v. 38)
Isn't that tremendous? All this ... in exchange for the keys of your life.
Can you afford to ignore the offer?

Watchman Nee, in his book *The Normal Christian Life* writes in chapter 10:

> 'Living in the Spirit means that I trust the Holy Spirit to do in me what I cannot do myself. This life is completely different from the life I would naturally live of myself. Each time I am faced with a new demand from the Lord, I look to Him to do in me what He requires of me.
>
> 'It is not a case of trying, but of trusting; not of struggling, but of resting in Him. If I have a hasty temper, impure thoughts, a quick tongue or a critical spirit, I shall not set out with a determined effort to change myself, but instead, reckoning myself dead in Christ to these things, I shall look to the Spirit of God to produce in me the needed purity or humility or meekness, confident that He will do so.'

* * *

I know you better than you do,
I made you.
Your thoughts are not secret,
Your desires cry out,
I hear them.
Security. Love. Freedom.
Only I can give them to you
body, mind and spirit.
I have a perfect plan for you.
Trust me.
I love you.
I am able.
I will provide your needs.
Yes, your needs,
not your wants.

Your wants are only superficial.
I know your heart – deep within you
I made you.
Don't be afraid.
It may be difficult.
But my strength – I give it you.
I go before you,
just follow me.
I will not give you something too
big for you,
I know your capabilities.
Stop fighting, my child, I made you.
Give me total control.
I love you.

JOY CROCOMBE.

'Bur when the Holy Spirit controls our lives, he will produce this kind of fruit in us: love, joy, peace, patience, kindness, goodness, faithfulness, gentleness and self-control' (Gal. 5:22, LB).

STUDY 7

WHAT ABOUT THE JEWS?

QUESTIONS

KEY THOUGHT: 'If the Jews abandon their unbelief, they will be put back in the place where they were, for God is able to do that.'

DAY 1 *Romans 9:1-18.*
a) Who is Paul writing about in verses 1-5?

b) Why is he sad about them?

c) What story is told here to show that God never promised to save people just because they were Jews?

DAY 2 *Romans 9:19-33.*
a) To whom did the prophecy in Hosea (vv. 25, 26) refer?

b) How were the Gentiles put right with God?

c) How were the Jews mistakenly trying to get right with God?

DAY 3 *Romans 10:1-13.*
a) What is the only way that a person (Jew or Gentile) can be saved?

b) – CHECK POINT– Have you done these two things? What did Paul tell the Philippian jailer in Acts 16:30, 31?

QUESTIONS (contd.)

DAY 4   *Romans 10:14-21.*

a) To be saved, a person must ....

b) To believe, he must ....

c) To hear the message, it must be ....

d) If someone is to proclaim the message, they must be ....

e) What do these verses suggest to you about missionary work?

DAY 5   *Romans 11:1-12.*

a) What is the proof that God has not totally rejected the Jews?

b) What happened as a result of the Jews' sin of rejection?

DAY 6   *Romans 11:13-24.*

a) What does it mean to 'graft' the branch of one tree on to the stem of another? Why is it done?

b) Who are likened here to the wild olive branch? and to the stem?

c) What warning is given in verse 20?

DAY 7   *Romans 11:25-36.*

a) In what way are the Jews enemies of God?

b) And in what way are they beloved of God? (v. 28)

c) What things does Paul marvel at?

NOTES

In Study 2 we saw that God chose Abraham to be the father of the Jewish race, God's chosen people. We saw also that Abraham was put right with God on the basis of his FAITH, and he lived years before the Law was given to Moses. God's plans are thoroughly consistent, for all through Old Testament history He has shown that there is only ONE WAY to be saved.

Yet after the Law was given, many of the Jews rejected God's plan of salvation by faith, and tried to win merit in His sight by keeping the Law. Others distorted His commands and turned to their own ways. But all along, we find there was a minority group who trusted God and were saved because of their faith.

When God sent Jesus into the world to take the penalty for the sin of mankind, Jesus came to His own people (the Jews), and His own people did not receive Him. As a nation, they rejected and had Him killed.

Then God chose Paul, a zealous Jew, to carry the message to the Gentiles, who, up till this time, had never had the gospel preached to them. Acts chapters 10 and 11 tell us what a revolutionary idea that seemed to the early (Hebrew) Christians at first! On Paul's first missionary journey, God's plan reached its climax. At a meeting in the synagogue, the Jews argued with Paul about his message and insulted him. He spoke out boldly:

'It was necessary that the word of God should be spoken first to you. But since you reject it and do not consider yourselves worthy of eternal life, we will leave you and go to the Gentiles' (Acts 13:46).

So the offer of salvation spread around the Gentile world, where it was received with joy. The branches of the original olive-tree stem had been broken off, but the new shoots from the wild olive were grafted in, and they flourished and produced fruit.

Yet Paul asserts here in Romans 11 that God's rejection of the Jews did not represent His final purpose, it was the punishment for their unbelief. And one reason for salvation coming to the Gentiles is that it should make the Jews realise what they have missed. Ultimately, God's chosen people will abandon their unbelief, and will be put back in the place where they were, for God is able to do that.

As we think back over this study, surely we must join with Paul when he says:

'I stand amazed at the fathomless wealth of God's wisdom and God's knowledge. How could man ever understand His reasons for action, or explain His methods of working?' (ch. 11:33, Phillips).

STUDY 8

'LORD, CHANGE ME!'

QUESTIONS

KEY THOUGHT: (*It will be very worthwhile if you read this verse aloud every day this week*) 'Let God transform you inwardly by a complete change of your mind, then you will be able to know the will of God.'

DAY 1   *Romans 12:1-2* (read in several different versions).
a) What do you think Paul means by 'a living sacrifice'?

b) In verse 2, what are we told not to do?

c) How will God change (or transform) us if we make ourselves available to Him?

DAY 2   *Romans 12:3-8.*
a) If we allow God to change (or renew) our minds, what kind of opinion will we have of ourselves?

b) What are we told in these verses about the people in a church fellowship?

DAY 3   *Romans 12:9-13.*
Make a list of the rules for Christian living given here. Then take each one thoughtfully in turn, and ask God to show you what changes need to be made in your life.

QUESTIONS (contd.)

DAY 4   *Romans 12:14-21.*
a) Which of these instructions do you find the most difficult to follow?

b) Why should we never give 'tit-for-tat'?

DAY 5   *Romans 13:1-7.*
a) What reasons are given here as to why we should obey the government?

b) Discuss how binding this is for Christians when the authorities conflict with what God commands (see Mark 12:17; Acts 5:29).

DAY 6   *Romans 13:8-10; Matthew 22:34-40.*
a) What single guiding principle should control the Christian's life in society?

b) Read 1 John 4:8 and 2 Corinthians 3 the end of verse 18 together. For what purpose does the Holy Spirit work in our lives to change (or transform) us?

DAY 7   *Romans 13:11-14.*
a) What reason is given here why we should be concerned about the quality of our Christian life?

b) Read chapter 12:2 again. What will result from God transforming us and changing our attitudes?

NOTES

Are you willing?

Read the key thought for this week again, and ask yourself: 'Am I willing?'

Not being willing is probably one of the greatest obstacles to growth in a Christian's life. And the older we get, the harder it is to be willing to let God change us. We get used to our own 'little ways' and shortcomings, and rationalize our failure to live as He has shown us.

Has this study shown you something in your life that needs changing? If it hasn't, you must be just about perfect!

* * *

We could almost say that chapters 9–11 (last week's study) were an 'aside' to the main flow of thought in this letter. What Paul is writing in chapter 12 seems to carry straight on from what he wrote at the end of chapter 8.

Notice especially chapter 8:29 which reads, 'Those whom God had already chosen, He set apart **to become like His Son.**'

Have you read the book, *Lord, change me* by Evelyn Christenson (published by Victor Books)? Chapters 1 and 2 give the warm, personal story of what happened when the author took Romans 12:2 literally, for herself. It is so easy to pray, 'Lord, change my wife', or 'my husband', or other people, but this week's study must be taken personally and individually.

* * *

Discovering what God wants me to do.

'How do I find out God's will for my life?'

'How do I know what God wants me to do? If I knew what it was, I'd be happy to do it. But how do I know?'

Do these questions sound familiar?

Books have been written with guidelines on how to know the will of God, but this chapter tells us clearly where to begin:

1. Hand over your life to Him and allow Him to work in you – and He promises that you will know what He wants you to do.
2. Look at yourself carefully, evaluate the abilities He has given you and ensure that you are using them, Romans 12:3-8.
3. Follow the straightforward directions in Romans 12:9-21, and as you do, His way will become clear.

Someone has said, 'It's not the parts of the Bible that I **don't** understand that worry me, it's the parts I do understand!'

There is so much of God's word that gives us clear guidelines on living. As we offer our bodies to Him as a living sacrifice, let us ask the Holy Spirit to take control, to renew our minds, and to reproduce Christ in our lives.

Can you sincerely pray this prayer?

> O Jesus, Lord and Saviour,
> I give myself to Thee,
> For Thou, in Thine atonement
> Didst give Thyself for me;
> I own no other Master,
> My heart shall be Thy throne,
> My life I give
> Henceforth to live
> O Christ, for Thee alone.

STUDY 9

QUESTIONS

KEY THOUGHT: (*Why not write this out and pin it up above the kitchen sink, or on your office desk?*) 'We must always aim at those things that bring peace, and that help to strengthen one another.'

DAY 1   *Romans 14:1-6; Colossians 2:16-17*
a) What challenged you most in last week's study?

b. What were the two points of disagreement amongst the Christians in Rome?

DAY 2   *Romans 14:5, 7-12; I Corinthians 10:31.*
a) What advice does Paul give on these differences of opinion?

b) What reason is given why people should follow this advice?

DAY 3   *Romans 14:13-18; Matthew 18:6.*
a) In relation to other Christians, what should be our aim in the way we live?

b) In relation to God, what should be our aim?

QUESTIONS (contd.)

DAY 4 *Romans 14:19-23; 1 Corinthians 9:19.*
a) Give an example of a situation today where you would need to be guided by verse 21.

b) If you yourself have doubts as to whether something is right for you (as a Christian) to do, how can you find out if it is?

DAY 5 *Romans 15:1-6.*
a) What proofs have we that Christ did not please Himself (see Mark 6:31-34; John 10:18; Matt. 27:27-31; Phil. 2:5-8)?

b) Following His example, what are we urged to do in verse 5? Why?

DAY 6 *Romans 15:7-13.*
a) Christ became a servant to the Jews for two reasons. What were they? (read also Rom. 11:11)

b) What is Paul's prayer for the Gentiles? (and that includes us!)

DAY 7 *Romans 15:14-21; Acts 9:15-16.*
a) What was the special work to which Paul had been called?

b) What was his ambition as he travelled around?

Our foremost aim in life as Christians is to please God.

This is made very clear to us in the Bible.

'It is my ambition to **please Christ** in everything' (2 Cor. 5:9).
'We pray ... that as you have learned from us the way of life that **pleases God**, you may continue in it, and deepen your experience of it' (I Thess. 4:1).
'We ask God to fill you with the knowledge of His Will ... then you will be able to live as the Lord wants, and always do what **pleases Him**' (Col. 1:9, 10).
'The Scripture says that before Enoch was taken up, he had **pleased God**' (Heb. 11:5).
'This is my own dear Son, with Whom I **am pleased**' (Matt. 3:17).

HOW do we please God? By pleasing others, not ourselves.

- Julie and Paul would enjoy going away at weekends, but they are involved in their local Sunday School, so they make sure they are always there on Sunday mornings.
- Jack built up his record collection until he reached the point where he preferred to sit and listen to records rather than go out to the weekly prayer meeting. He prayed about this, and decided to limit his hobby to one night a week.
- Jan's girl friend is not a Christian. Jan would like to sing in the choir at the forthcoming Crusade, but realizes there is more chance of her friend coming to the meetings if she can sit with her, so she doesn't join.
- In Peter's local church, there is a meeting to decide whether choruses should be used in the morning service. Peter hates the idea, but does not force his opinion, because he sees that most of the others want to have them.
- Pam picks up four children every week and brings them to youth group. She usually has to wait for a few minutes at each house. It would be much easier to tell them she hasn't time to collect them. But she doesn't – she prays for patience, and gets on with the job for the Lord's sake.

Our lovely Example – 'Even Christ did not please Himself.'

Listen to His own words:

'Here I am, O God, I have come to do what You want me to do' (Heb. 10:9).
'My food ... is to do the will of him who sent me' (John 4:34).
'Not my will, but yours be done' (Luke 22:42).

* * *

Has our key thought helped you to be an easier person to live with this week?

STUDY 10

REAL PEOPLE, LIKE US

QUESTIONS

KEY THOUGHT: 'May God, our source of peace, be with you all.'

DAY 1 *Romans 15:22-33.*
a) Paul is writing from Corinth. Where was he planning to go next?

Why?

b) Where will he go next?

DAY 2 *Romans 16:1-6, 12.*
a) What comments does Paul make about these women: Phoebe, Priscilla, Mary, Tryphena, Tryphosa and Persis?

b) What does this suggest about the place of women in the early church?

DAY 3 *Romans 16:7-11.*
a) What have Andronicus, Junias and Herodion in common?

b) How did Paul know all these people mentioned in this chapter, when he had never been to Rome?

QUESTIONS (contd.)

DAY 4 *Romans 16:10-16, 3-5.*
a) Paul mentions 5 'households', 'families', 'groups of Christian brothers.' Can you spot them?

b) Discuss some practical ways in which Christians in the same household today can follow the instructions Paul gave in Romans 14:13; 15:1-2.

DAY 5 *Romans 16:17-23; I Corinthians 1:10-11.*
a) What warning does Paul give before closing this letter?

b) How do you think this letter would have helped those small groups of believers in Rome?

DAY 6 *Romans 16:25-27; 15:5-6.*
a) Who alone is able to make us stand firm in our faith?

b) How can we glorify God?

c) How is God described in chapter 15:5, 13, 33, and 16:27?

DAY 7 Read again all the 'KEY THOUGHTS' that we have had in Romans.
a) How many of them can you say by heart?

b) How would you briefly summarize the main teaching of this Book?

NOTES

If Paul's friend had had a camera, they might have sent him a photo of these men and women in Rome who loved the Lord! Wouldn't it be interesting to know what they looked like?

However, they didn't have a camera, so we must use our imagination. But of course their outward appearance is not important, because God looks on the heart; and what really matters about these people (and about you and me) is how they lived their lives.

Let's have a look at them going about their daily work.

PHOEBE is a generous and helpful lady, working as a deaconess for the Christians at Cenchrea (near Corinth). She will be travelling soon, to take this letter of Paul to Rome.

PRISCILLA and AQUILA, now living in Rome, first met Paul on an earlier visit to Corinth (Acts 18:1-3). Priscilla was probably a Roman lady of noble birth, and her husband was a Jew who worked at the same trade as Paul: tent-making. I wonder what the frightening incident was, in which they risked their lives for him.

EPENETUS must have lived in Asia (now Turkey) when Paul began his missionary journeys. What a thrill it was for Paul when this man realized that he could be put right with God by faith alone, and he became the first Christian in that region. Now he is living in Rome, and we can imagine how eagerly he would share Christ with those he met.

ANDRONICUS and JUNIAS were Jews. They had been believers in the Lord longer than Paul had. They were obviously leaders in the church, and they had suffered with Paul in prison. What a bond of friendship there would be between them! I'm sure they would have been encouraged to read what Paul had written about the Jewish nation in this letter.

RUFUS is interesting to think about. Mark must have written his gospel around this time, and when he mentions how Simon of Cyrene carried the cross for Jesus, he identifies him as 'the father of Alexander and Rufus' (Mark 15:21), as if to say, 'you would know these brothers.' Mark's gospel would have been first read by the Christians in Rome, so it seems likely that this Rufus was, in fact, the son of the man who carried Christ's cross. It is interesting to note that his mother had so lovingly cared for Paul.

So, all these and the other unfamiliar-sounding names stand for real people like us, living men and women who were serving the Lord in the great city of Rome. Can you appreciate how precious Christian fellowship was to them? How eagerly they would receive this letter from Paul, and how they would long for the day when he would visit them!

Paul wrote this in Corinth about AD 55, not many years before the grim date of July AD 64, when Rome went up in flames, and Emperor Nero, seeking a scapegoat for what was probably his own crime, savagely struck out at the Christians.

* * *

If Paul were writing this letter to us today, how might he conclude?

'Greetings to my dear friend Rob, who takes a personal interest in the young people in this area, to win them for Christ.

'Greetings also to Anne, a woman who is never too busy to listen to someone else's troubles.

'And to Mike, who gave his life to the Lord only a few years ago, and who now stands firm, even when his mates call him names.

'Greet dear Julie, who has many problems to cope with, and greet those who come to the Bible Study group in her home.'

What if your name were on the list? What would Paul write about you?

ANSWER GUIDE

The following pages contain an Answer Guide. It is recommended that answers to the questions be attempted before turning to this guide. It is only a guide and the answers given should not be treated as exhaustive.

LEADERS GUIDE

LEADERS – Read this first

Romans is acknowledged to be one of the most difficult books of the Bible to understand, We are not approaching this study as theological students might – savouring every verse and digging deeply into the wonderful truths – but rather, our aim is to make the overall message of this most important document intelligible to the people in our Bible Study groups.

So, leaders, please spend time making yourselves familiar with the key thought for each study, and centre the discussion on this as far as possible. Obviously, ten studies cannot probe the depths of a book like Romans, but God has a vital message for us all here, and we must not let anything hinder the message getting through. For this reason, key references are taken from the Good News Bible, where words like 'justified', 'righteousness', 'atonement' etc. are replaced by modern equivalents.

Allow yourself enough time each day to read and reread the passage, and let it simmer in your mind for the whole day. This is particularly important with a book like Romans.

William Tyndale, in 1534, commented on Romans:

'No man verily can read it too oft or study it too well: for the more it is studied the easier it is, the more it is chewed the pleasanter it is, and the more groundly it is searched the preciouser things are found in it, so great treasure of spiritual things lieth therein.'

In the Good News Bible, there is an excellent page of introduction to Romans. It is a masterly summary of the book, and will help you, as leader, to grasp the message of the study as a whole before you begin.

PRAY ... for understanding for your group, for wisdom and clarity of thought for yourself, and for a clear, uncluttered channel of thought for the Holy Spirit to come through.

GUIDE TO INTRODUCTORY STUDY

The purpose of this Introductory Study is twofold:

1. To read and understand Romans 1:1-17 (as Study 1 begins at v. 18).
2. To help each member of the group to realise that even the 'good' people are sinful and need a Saviour.

Try to get the book, *Basic Christianity* by John Stott (I.V.P. Publication), and read chapter 5, 'The fact and nature of sin'. This is an excellent book of Christian doctrine for your bookshelf.

Some references for you to look up beforehand. They may help to get your thinking clear about sin.

1 Kings 8:46; Psalm 14:1-3; Psalm 130:3; Ecclesiastes 7:20; Isaiah 53:6; Matthew 5:21, 22, 27, 28; Romans 3:23; James 4:17; 1 John 1:8, 10; 1 John 3:4

The fact of sin is borne out, not only by the Bible, but by our newspapers, by our experience, and by the legislation which our country needs.

There are two aspects of sin:

POSITIVE – a moral law we break
NEGATIVE – perfection that we fail to reach

A SUGGESTION

The Living Bible translates 1 Timothy 2:5:

'God is on one side, and all the people on the other side, and Christ Jesus, Himself man, is between them to bring them together.'

Having established the fact of universal sin through the discussion, you may like to use this verse to illustrate the one and only hope for mankind. A simple diagram, prepared beforehand, would help your group to get a picture of this great truth.

GUIDE TO STUDY 1

DAY 1 a) The ability that God has given man to see Himself in the things He has created.

b) God's anger upon them, they have no excuse for not honouring God, their minds are filled with darkness, they are fools, they choose to believe lies, they worship and serve 'things' rather than God. (Point out how these can apply to 'civilized' people today.)

DAY 2 a) Discussion.

b) They deliberately refuse to acknowledge God. (Phillips gives a graphic translation of verses 28-31.)

DAY 3 a) Repentance.

b) Perfection.

DAY 4 a) Verse 23.

b) That he was a sinner.

DAY 5 a) Circumcision.

b) The person whose heart has been 'circumcised' (i.e. put right with God by having sin 'cut away').

c) A changed heart and a new relationship with Himself.

DAY 6 a) He entrusted His message to them; He chose them to be His special people, His sons; He gave them His laws (rules), His promises (covenants), and the true way to worship Him; They had a glorious ancestry, Jesus the Messiah was born into their nation.

b) Some of them were unfaithful to God.

c) Although the Jews as a nation were God's chosen people, not all were real Jews.

DAY 7 a) That everyone has sinned, and falls short of God's standard of perfection.

b) So that we might be conscious of how far we fall short.

GUIDE TO STUDY 2

DAY 1 a) Personal
b) Faith in Jesus Christ and what He has done for us

DAY 2 a) How good we are, or how well we have kept God's law.
b) When God gave the Law, He commanded that it should be remembered from generation to generation. Also, Christ made it clear that the law in no way conflicted with His teachings.

DAY 3 a) Because of his faith, i.e., because he trusted in God. Yes. (Jesus Christ is God.)
b) Wages are a reward for work, but a gift is entirely due to the benevolence of the giver.

DAY 4 a) By being put right with God (accepted by God) and therefore having his sins forgiven.
b) Personal.
c) All those who put their trust in Christ.

DAY 5 a) Then faith is meaningless, and God's promise (e.g. our key thought for this week) is not true.
b) He is a father in the spiritual sense, in matters of faith, because he was justified by faith.

DAY 6 a) Personal. (He was absolutely sure that God would be able to do what He had promised, GNB v. 21.)
b) Because God had promised a physical impossibility.

DAY 7 a) He was instituting a divine principle which would apply to us as well, and to everyone who trusts in God for salvation.
b) Because of our sin.
c) To put us right with God.

GUIDE TO STUDY 3

DAY 1   a) We have peace with God, through our Lord Jesus Christ.
b) Sharing the glory of God. (Point out that 'hope' when used in the Bible, means a 'confident looking forward'.)

DAY 2   a) Because suffering produces endurance, endurance produces strength of character (GNB, God's approval) and character, hope.
b) Read verse 5b in several versions to get an overall picture.

DAY 3   a) Powerless (helpless, weak); wicked (ungodly, sinful); sinners; enemies of God.
b) Share these verses with them! (**Leaders**, draw out from your group the full meaning of verse 8.)

DAY 4   a) He has made it possible for us to be put right with (or reconciled to, or made friends with) God.
b) Personal.

DAY 5   a) Through Adam's disobedience. God created man with free will to choose or disobey.
b) Death. (Read 'Basic Christianity', chapter 5, if possible again.)

DAY 6   a) Adam's sin and God's free gift.
b) Adam's sin brought judgment, condemnation, a verdict of 'guilty', whereas God's free gift brought justification, acquittal, a verdict of 'not guilty'. (LB: death and life.)

DAY 7   a) God's grace increased all the more.
b) Answers to this question will be personal, and perhaps imaginative, but also link it with the teaching in this chapter. Ephesians 2:1-3 and 12, would also be helpful.

ROMANS • ANSWER GUIDE • • • •

49

GUIDE TO STUDY 4

DAY 1
a) 'Should we not keep on sinning, so that we can experience more and more of God's grace and forgiveness?'
b) 'Of course not. We have died to sin, so this is unthinkable.'

DAY 2
a) He doesn't react at all!
b) 1) That our old self with its sinful desires, was put to death on the cross with Him.
2) That we have been raised to a new kind of life.

DAY 3
a) He died once and cannot die again; He died to sin and was raised from the dead, death has no more power over Him.
b) Dead to sinful desires, and alive to God.

DAY 4
a) We must not allow sin to control our bodies, not give in to our sinful desires, and not let any part of ourselves be used 'as weapons of evil for the devil's purposes' (Phillips).
b) It is to give ourselves completely to God, so that He can use us for His purposes.

DAY 5
a) That of a master who owns a slave and demands obedience from him.
b) Personal (e.g. drug addiction, drink, the occult, etc.).

DAY 6
a) That the Christian, through what Christ did for him, is free from the power of sin.
b) Personal.
c) To surrender ourselves entirely as slaves of righteousness.

DAY 7
a) righteousness; death; the power of sin; eternal life
b) Personal.

GUIDE TO STUDY 5

DAY 1   a) 'Till death us do part' – until one partner dies.
b) The other is free from that vow, and may marry again.

DAY 2   a) A legalistic obedience to the Law out of a sense of duty.
b) On the hearts of God's people. They would know the Lord in a personal relationship, and obey Him because they loved Him.

DAY 3   a) No.
b) The 10th. Personal.

DAY 4   a) It is holy, just and good, it does not contradict God's promises. The Law was the teacher and guide to lead people to Christ.
b) Because there is sin in our nature, which opposes what is good.

DAY 5   a) He can only do what he doesn't want to do!
b) See 'key thought' for this week. Our human nature and the Holy Spirit within us are constantly opposed to each other, each seeking to have control of us (see Rom. 8:5).

DAY 6   a) After (some commentators say before).
b) Verse 25. Jesus Christ Himself is the answer.

DAY 7   a) The Law.
b) He realises his sin.
c) To please God. No.

GUIDE TO STUDY 6

DAY 1 a) Verse 2.
b) God did what the Law couldn't do; He put into effect a plan to save us.
Jesus came as a sin-offering to satisfy the demands of the Law.
The Holy Spirit brings life, and sets us free from the law of sin and death.

DAY 2 a) those who live as human nature tells them to, and those who live as the
Spirit tells them to.
b) death; life and peace
c) Eternal life is synonymous with having the Spirit of Christ (Romans) and
with having the Son of God in I John. (This is not a contradiction. Think about
it!)

DAY 3 a) Sons of God, heirs of God the Father and joint-heirs with Christ the Son.
b) The Holy Spirit.

DAY 4 a) When compared with the future glory, present sufferings pale into
insignificance, and are temporary.
b) Waiting for God to set it free from curse and decay.

DAY 5 a) The hope of a new heaven and new earth, where pain and suffering will be
no more.
b) The Holy Spirit. (If possible, read out verses 26 and 27 from the New
English Bible.)
c) Personal.

DAY 6 a) Personal.
b) That we should become like His Son (v. 29).

DAY 7 a) Nobody. (If Satan is given as the answer, remember that Christ is stronger
than Satan.)
b) Nobody.
c) Nobody.
d) Personal.

GUIDE TO STUDY 7

DAY 1
a) The Jews.
b) Because as a nation they rejected Jesus.
c) Jacob and Esau – Jacob pleased God and was saved, Esau was not.

DAY 2
a) The Gentiles (non Jews).
b) Through faith.
c) Through the Law.

DAY 3
a) Verse 9. 'Believe on the Lord Jesus Christ and you will be saved.'
b) Tell others with your own mouth that Jesus Christ is your Lord, and believe in your heart that God has raised Him from the dead.

DAY 4
a) Believe
b) Hear the message
c) Proclaimed
d) Sent
e) Personal.

DAY 5
a) There has always been a small number who have been faithful to Him.
b) Salvation came to the Gentiles.

DAY 6
a) To insert the branch into the stem and attach it firmly, so that it will get nourishment from the stem and grow. To produce better fruit
b) The Gentiles. The Jewish nation.
c) That the Gentiles should not arrogantly boast of God's favour to them.

DAY 7
a) They are enemies because they reject the gospel, but friends of God because of His promise to Abraham.
b) God's riches, wisdom, knowledge, decisions and ways.

NOTE FOR LEADERS: Scholars differ in their interpretation of Romans 11:25-29. For this reason, the passage has not been highlighted in these notes. You will find helpful comments in the Tyndale Commentary (pp. 220-223), for your own further study.

GUIDE TO STUDY 8

DAY 1 a) In the old covenant the dead animal was presented to God on an altar, as a gift to Him. In the new covenant Jesus' human body was offered as a final and complete sacrifice for sin. God asks us to present our bodies to Him, but He wants us alive, so that He can use us in His service.

b) Not to model ourselves on the behaviour of the world around us (Jerusalem Bible). (See also Phillips.)

c) Inwardly, by a complete change of mind, or attitude.

DAY 2 a) An honest and modest opinion, not exaggerating our own importance.

b) Each person has a different gift to be used in the building up of the fellowship.

DAY 3 Love must be sincere.

Hate anything evil, stand for what is good.

Have a real, warm affection for one another.

Show respect for one another (i.e., be willing to let the other person have the credit).

Don't be lazy, work hard.

Serve the Lord enthusiastically.

Base your happiness on your hope in Christ.

Be patient in trouble.

Be prayerful always.

Share what you have with God's people.

Open your home for hospitality.

(**Leaders**, if some of your group have not thought these over carefully at home, read them out one by one with a silent pause in between.)

DAY 4 a) Personal. (LB makes these verses vivid!)

b) Because God will avenge any evil Himself.

DAY 5 a) Those who exercise authority on earth, do so by delegation from God. To disobey them is to disobey God. If we go against the law, we'll be punished, and we'll be acting against our conscience.

b) Discussion.

DAY 6 a) Love.

b) To make us more like the Lord, who Himself is Love.

DAY 7 a) Because the day of the Lord's return could be any time now.

b) We will be increasingly able to know the will of God.

GUIDE TO STUDY 9

DAY 1   a) Personal.

b) 1) Food – Whether or not to eat meat (that had previously been consecrated to pagan gods. For your own personal study, read I Corinthians 8 and the Tyndale Commentary (pp. 246-251). However, with your group, don't spend too long on this – rather concentrate on the principle behind this week's study – i.e., avoiding things that might weaken another Christian's faith.)

2) The religious observance of certain days.

DAY 2   a) We should be sure in our own minds about what we are doing, that the purpose of it is to glorify God and not to satisfy our own desires.

b) Because one day each of us will stand before God, and it is to Him alone that we shall have to answer for our actions.

DAY 3   a) To live in such a way that we never put a stumbling-block or obstacle in a fellow-Christian's way.

b) To please Him in everything we do.

DAY 4   a) Personal. (Notice that it is not only situations relating to food and drink, but also to 'anything else that would make your brother stumble.' Again, centre the discussion on the underlying principle.)

b) Verse 23 answers this. (NEB translates it clearly.) Other suggestions may be added – discussion with a mature Christian, prayer, the Holy Spirit's guidance, etc.

DAY 5   a) He sometimes didn't have time to eat; gave up sleep so that He could pray; laid down His life; was humiliated and tortured; left the glories of heaven and became man.

b) Live in complete harmony with other Christians. So that together we may truly glorify God.

DAY 6   a) To show that God is true to His promises to the Jews; so that the Gentiles might be saved and glorify God.

b) That God may fill us with joy, peace and hope.

DAY 7   a) To be a servant of Christ Jesus to work for the Gentiles.

b) To bring the gospel to places where the very name of Christ had not been heard.

GUIDE TO STUDY 10

You may also like to read the 'notes' in sections alongside the appropriate days on the question sheet.

DAY 1 Jerusalem. An offering had been given by the believers in Macedonia and Achaia for the Christians in Jerusalem, and Paul was going to take it to them. To Rome, and then to Spain. (It is essential to bring along a map to show your group the relative distances.)

DAY 2 a) Phoebe has worked hard in the church;
     Priscilla has been a fellow-worker;
     Mary has worked so hard;
     Tryphena and Tryphosa (twins?) are the Lord's workers;
     and Persis has worked hard.
     b) That they were an active and vital part of the Lord's work.

DAY 3 a) They were Jews.
     b) He had met them in other places, and they had since moved to the great capital of the Empire.

DAY 4 a) Verses 5, 10, 11, 14, 15. (N.B.. 'The church' in the first century had no buildings specially built for worship. 'The church that met in their house' could be likenend to our Bible Study groups.)
     b) Discussion.

DAY 5 a) To watch out for people who cause divisions and try to upset people's faith.
     b) It would have given them a strong principle of doctrine to stick to, and pointed them to true freedom which comes only through the Holy Spirit's control (Has it helped us in this way?)

DAY 6 a) God.
     b) By agreeing together about Him, by following the example of Jesus, by praising and worshipping Him.
     c) The source of patience and encouragement; the source of hope; our source of peace; all-wise (GNB).

DAY 7 a) Personal.
     b) Personal.

NOTES

NOTES

OLD TESTAMENT

Triumphs Over Failures: A Study in Judges ISBN 1-85792-888-1 (above left)
Messenger of Love: A Study in Malachi ISBN 1-85792-885-7 (above right)
The Beginning of Everything: A Study in Genesis 1-11 ISBN 0-90806-728-3
Hypocrisy in Religion: A Study in Amos ISBN 0-90806-706-2
Unshakeable Confidence: A Study in Habakkuk & Joel ISBN 0-90806-751-8
A Saviour is Promised: A Study in Isaiah 1 - 39 ISBN 0-90806-755-0
The Throne and Temple: A Study in 1 & 2 Chronicles ISBN 1-85792-910-1
Our Magnificent God: A Study in Isaiah 40 - 66 ISBN 1-85792-909-8
The Cost of Obedience: A Study in Jeremiah ISBN 0-90806-761-5
Focus on Faith: A Study of 10 Old Testament Characters ISBN 1-85792-890-3
Faith, Courage and Perserverance: A Study in Ezra ISBN 1-85792-949-7

NEW TESTAMENT

The World's Only Hope: A Study in Luke ISBN 1-85792-886-5 (above left)
Walking in Love: A Study in John's Epistles ISBN 1-85792-891-1 (above right)
Faith that Works: A Study in James ISBN 0-90806-701-1
Made Completely New: A Study in Colossians & Philemon ISBN 0-90806-721-6
Jesus-Christ, Who is He? A Study in John's Gospel ISBN 0-90806-716-X
Entering by Faith: A Study in Hebrews ISBN 1-85792-914-4
Heavenly Living: A Study in Ephesians ISBN 1-85792-911-X
The Early Church: A Study in Acts 1-12 ISBN 0-90806-736-4
Get Ready: A Study in 1 & 2 Thessalonians ISBN 1-85792-948-9

CHARACTERS

Abraham: A Study of Genesis 12-25 ISBN 1-85792-887-3 (above left)
Serving the Lord: A Study of Joshua ISBN 1-85792-889-X (above right)
Achieving the Impossible: A Study of Nehemiah ISBN 0-90806-707-0
God plans for Good: A Study of Joseph ISBN 0-90806-700-3
A Man After God's Own Heart: A Study of David ISBN 0-90806-746-1
Grace & Grit: A Study of Ruth & Esther ISBN 1-85792-908-X
Men of Courage: A Study of Elijah & Elisha ISBN 1-85792-913-6
Meek but Mighty: A Study of Moses ISBN 1-85792-951-9

THEMES

God's Heart, My Heart: World Mission ISBN 1-85792-892-X (above left)
Freedom: You Can Find it! ISBN 0-90806-702-X (above right)
Freely Forgiven: A Study in Redemption ISBN 0-90806-720-8
The Problems of Life! Is there an Answer? ISBN 1-85792-907-1
Understanding the Way of Salvation ISBN 0-90082-880-3
Saints in Service: 12 Bible Characters ISBN 1-85792-912-8
Finding Christ in the Old Testament: Pre-existence and Prophecy
ISBN 0-90806-739-9

THE WORD WORLDWIDE

We first heard of WORD WORLDWIDE over 20 years ago when Marie Dinnen, its founder, shared excitedly about the wonderful way ministry to one needy woman had exploded to touch many lives. It was great to see the Word of God being made central in the lives of thousands of men and women, then to witness the life-changing results of them applying the Word to their circumstances. Over the years the vision for WORD WORLDWIDE has not dimmed in the hearts of those who are involved in this ministry. God is still at work through His Word and in today's self-seeking society, the Word is even more relevant to those who desire true meaning and purpose in life. WORD WORLDWIDE is a ministry of WEC International, an interdenominational missionary society, whose sole purpose is to see Christ known, loved and worshipped by all, particularly those who have yet to hear of His wonderful name. This ministry is a vital part of our work and we warmly recommend the WORD WORLDWIDE 'Geared for Growth' Bible studies to you. We know that as you study His Word you will be enriched in your personal walk with Christ. It is our hope that as you are blessed through these studies, you will find opportunities to help others discover a personal relationship with Jesus. As a mission we would encourage you to work with us to make Christ known to the ends of the earth.

Stewart and Jean Moulds – British Directors, **WEC International.**

A full list of over 50 'Geared for Growth' studies can be obtained from:

John and Ann Edwards
5 Louvaine Terrace, Hetton-le-Hole, Tyne & Wear, DH5 9PP
Tel. 0191 5262803 Email: rhysjohn.edwards@virgin.net

Anne Jenkins
2 Windermere Road, Carnforth, Lancs., LA5 9AR
Tel. 01524 734797 Email: anne@jenkins.abelgratis.com

UK Website: www.gearedforgrowth.co.uk

Christian Focus Publications

publishes books for all ages

Our mission statement –

STAYING FAITHFUL

In dependence upon God we seek to help make His infallible word, the Bible, relevant. Our aim is to ensure that the Lord Jesus Christ is presented as the only hope to obtain forgiveness of sin, live a useful life and look forward to heaven with Him.

REACHING OUT

Christ's last command requires us to reach out to our world with His gospel. We seek to help fulfil that by publishing books that point people towards Jesus and help them develop a Christ-like maturity. We aim to equip all levels of readers for life, work, ministry and mission.

Books in our adult range are published in three imprints.

Christian Focus contains popular works including biographies, commentaries, basic doctrine, and Christian living. Our children's books are also published in this imprint.

Mentor focuses on books written at a level suitable for Bible College and seminary students, pastors, and other serious readers; the imprint includes commentaries, doctrinal studies, examination of current issues, and church history.

Christian Heritage contains classic writings from the past.

For details of our titles visit us on our website
www.christianfocus.com

Christian Focus Publications, Ltd
Geanies House, Fearn,
Ross-shire, IV20 ITW, Scotland, United Kingdom
info@christianfocus.com